The Beatles

SADDLEBACK
EDUCATIONAL PUBLISHING

Saddleback's Graphic Biographies

SADDLEBACK
EDUCATIONAL PUBLISHING
www.sdlback.com

ISBN-13: 978-1-59905-216-8
ISBN-10: 1-59905-216-4
eBook: 978-1-60291-579-4

Printed in Guangzhou, China
0112/CA21200024

16 15 14 13 12   4 5 6 7 8 9

"The thing is, we're all really the same person. We're just four parts of the one." Paul McCartney

The Beatles charted 20 number one singles in the United States—three more than Elvis.

Liverpool is the industrial city in England where the Beatles grew up. In those days there were more people out of work there than in any other place in the country.

Merseyside was a section of Liverpool. It had many clubs where small bands played for teenagers. As many as 350 bands played there for very little money.

The *Mersey Beat* was a newspaper known only to local beat music lovers until the Beatles made Liverpool, and the newspaper, famous.

Liverpool had one of the first rock concerts. Alan Williams, the Beatles first manager, held a fourteen hour pop concert outdoors.

Williams also owned the Jacaranda and the Cavern Club where the Beatles played.

John Lennon

Stay until the baby is born.

John Lennon was born in October 1940. His father came and went from his life frequently.

John went to live with his aunt and uncle when he was about 5 years old.

See, Aunt Mimi, I've written a story for you. And I drew a picture too.

John liked to draw. He also enjoyed listening to music.

When John was eleven, he heard Bill Haley and the Comets on records. Then he discovered the records of Elvis Presley.

Are you listening to "Rock Around the Clock" again?

No, something I just got. A singer named Elvis Presley. He's American and great!

I'm glad you came to see me. I want to ask a favor, Mum. Could you buy me a guitar?

Well, Luv, if I can find an inexpensive one, it's yours.

A guitar's all right, John, but you'll never earn a living from it.

When he was sixteen, John formed a musical group called the Quarrymen. In 1958 his mother was killed by a car. An unhappy John was comforted by his friend Paul McCartney.

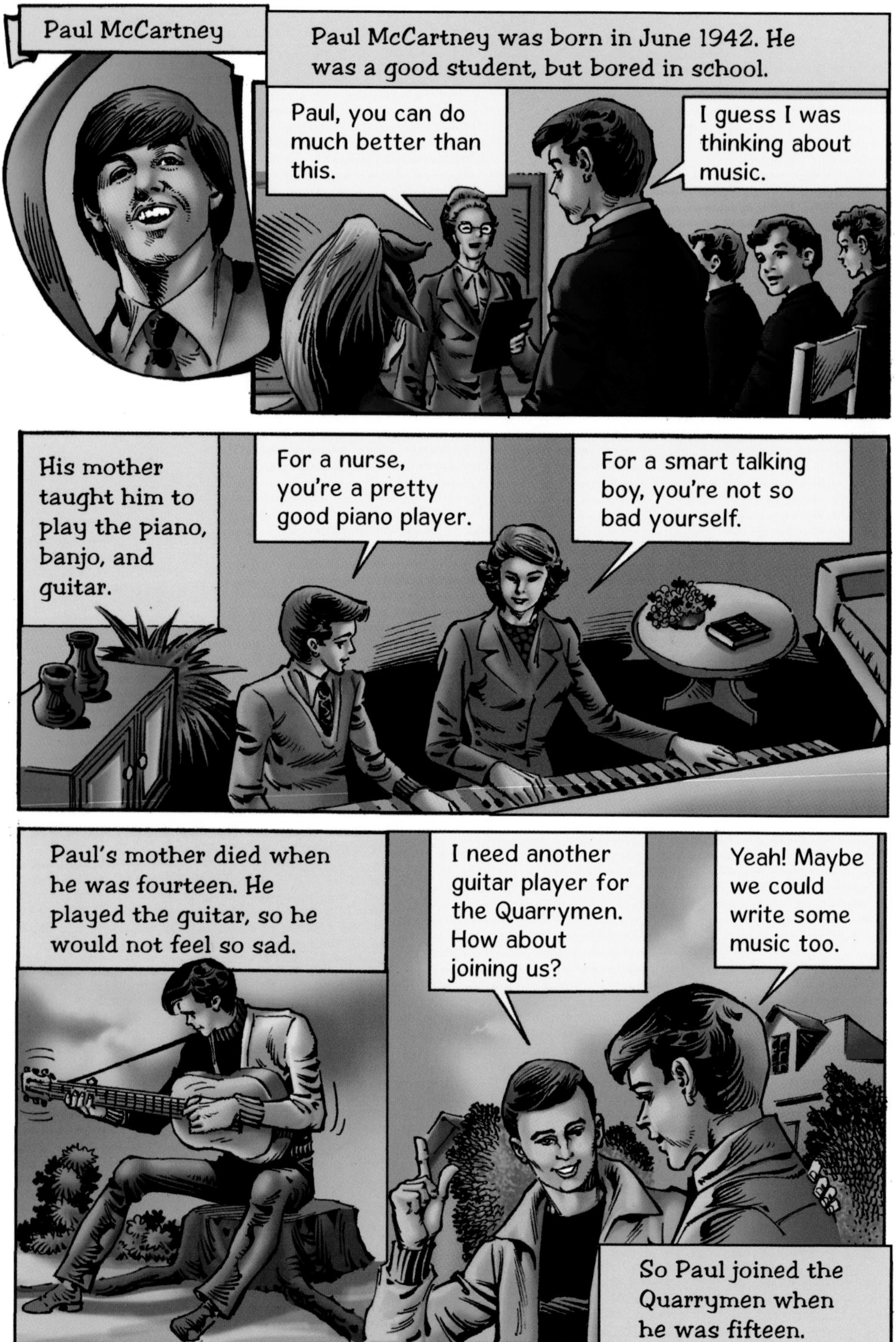
Paul McCartney
Paul McCartney was born in June 1942. He was a good student, but bored in school.
Paul, you can do much better than this.
I guess I was thinking about music.
His mother taught him to play the piano, banjo, and guitar.
For a nurse, you're a pretty good piano player.
For a smart talking boy, you're not so bad yourself.
Paul's mother died when he was fourteen. He played the guitar, so he would not feel so sad.
I need another guitar player for the Quarrymen. How about joining us?
Yeah! Maybe we could write some music too.
So Paul joined the Quarrymen when he was fifteen.

George Harrison

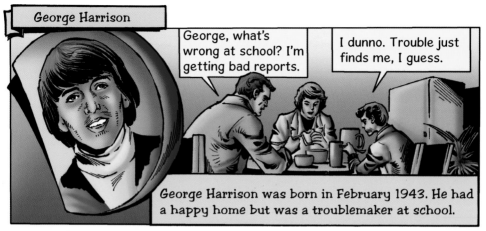

George, what's wrong at school? I'm getting bad reports.

I dunno. Trouble just finds me, I guess.

George Harrison was born in February 1943. He had a happy home but was a troublemaker at school.

In his teens, George was a British "teddy boy," a tough guy.

My folks are great. But I've got to be independent.

My folks don't care if I'm alive or dead.

It took you a long time to get interested in music.

Yeah, but I am now. I'm going to ask mum for a guitar.

George isn't too young for us. I wasn't much older when I joined last year.

He's mighty good on that guitar. So, okay George.

George had no interest in music until he was fourteen. Then Paul McCartney helped him learn to play the guitar.

George joined the Quarrymen in 1958.

John changed the name of the Quarrymen to the Silver Beatles then to the Beatles. The "beat" in Beatles stood for beat music.

The Beatles played at many of the clubs at Merseyside. John, Paul, and George were joined by Stuart Sutcliffe on guitar and Tommy Moore on the drums.

In 1960 Allan Williams, their manager, got them a date to play at a music club in Hamburg, Germany. Tommy was replaced on the drums by Pete Best.

They're making so much noise. They can't hear us.

They don't understand the words in English anyway. Just pound the chords and scream the lyrics.

Okay, imitate the German soldier! March, march!

Let's all imitate the soldiers by high-stepping.

At their drinking and dancing clubs the Germans wanted loud music with a good beat. The Beatles gave them this.

The Germans loved to see the Beatles fool around and make fun of Hitler.

The Beatles were overtired, often playing for eight hours a day, seven days a week. They lived in run-down apartments behind the club where they performed.

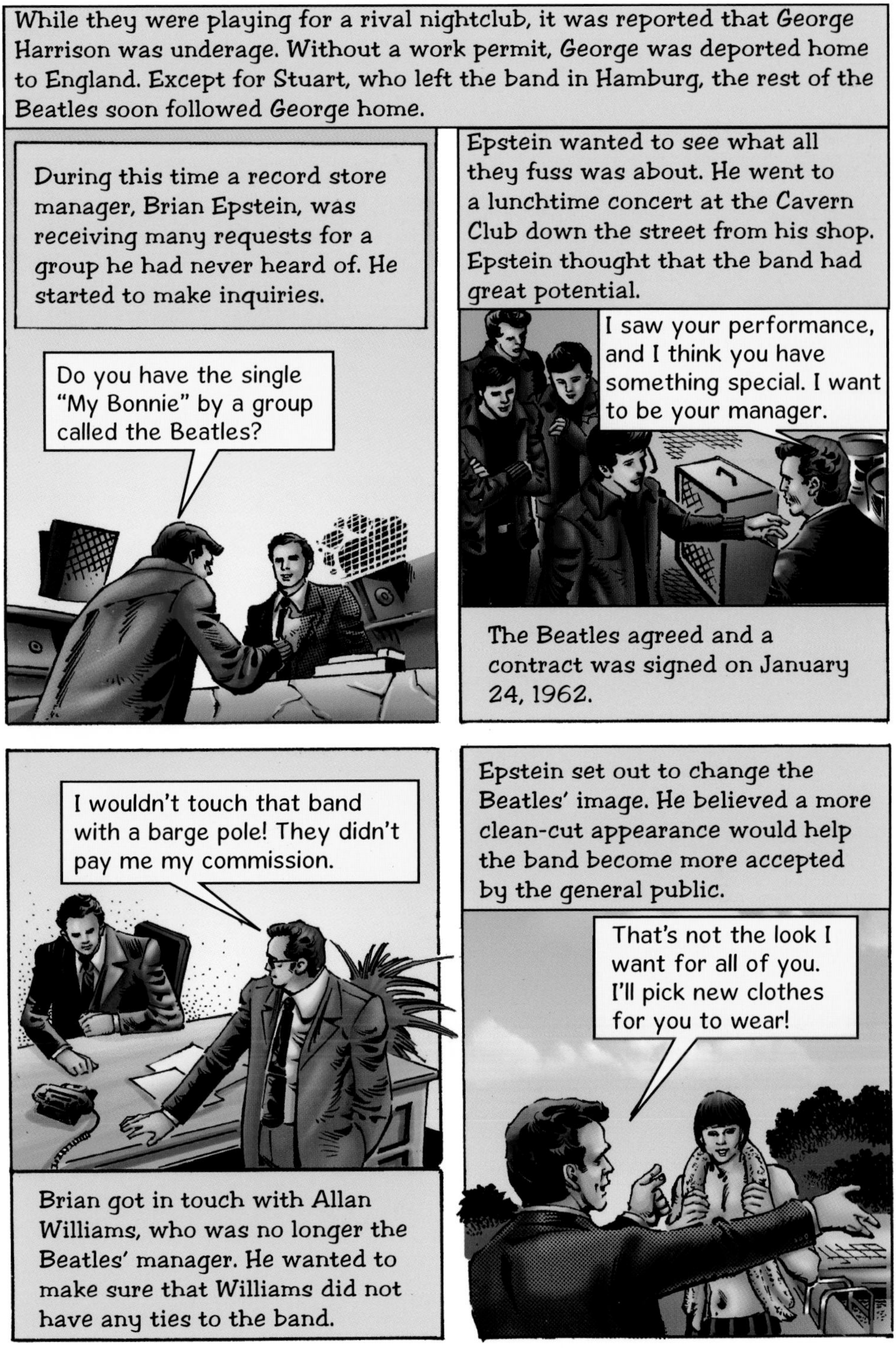
While they were playing for a rival nightclub, it was reported that George Harrison was underage. Without a work permit, George was deported home to England. Except for Stuart, who left the band in Hamburg, the rest of the Beatles soon followed George home.
During this time a record store manager, Brian Epstein, was receiving many requests for a group he had never heard of. He started to make inquiries.
Do you have the single "My Bonnie" by a group called the Beatles?
Epstein wanted to see what all they fuss was about. He went to a lunchtime concert at the Cavern Club down the street from his shop. Epstein thought that the band had great potential.
I saw your performance, and I think you have something special. I want to be your manager.
The Beatles agreed and a contract was signed on January 24, 1962.
I wouldn't touch that band with a barge pole! They didn't pay me my commission.
Brian got in touch with Allan Williams, who was no longer the Beatles' manager. He wanted to make sure that Williams did not have any ties to the band.
Epstein set out to change the Beatles' image. He believed a more clean-cut appearance would help the band become more accepted by the general public.
That's not the look I want for all of you. I'll pick new clothes for you to wear!

Epstein tried to interest several recording companies in the Beatles. They turned him down.

You should realize that the Beatles will be bigger than Presley.

Go back to your store business, Brian.

Finally Epstein persuaded George Martin of EMI to listen to the Beatles.

They have something! Yes, I'll be their recording manager.

John, Paul, and George began to be a little upset with Pete Best.

We're a group. Pete forgets that.

He acts like he's a one-man band.

Martin insisted that Pete Best did not fit into the group. Epstein liked Pete but had to let him go.

I'm sorry, Pete. But we have to do what EMI says.

I'll find work.

In August 1962 Ringo Starr became the Beatles' drummer. He was later called "the luckiest unknown drummer in the world." But as the fourth Beatle, Ringo Starr held his own with the others.

Ringo Starr

Ritchie Starkey was born in July 1940. He became Ringo Starr.

I wish I had a brother or sister to play with.

You're enough for us! But I wish we had a bathroom.

Due to several illnesses, Ringo was in and out of the hospital until he was a teenager.

He's still too weak to go home yet.

Ringo met the Beatles in Hamburg. He was playing with another group.

I live behind our club too. Those rooms are worse than these. I'll take the conditions in Liverpool any day.

Do you like Liverpool better because of a hairdresser named Maureen Cox?

Music groups had always recorded material written by someone else.

I can't find a song I like for the Beatles!

Martin let the Beatles record "Love Me Do," written by John and Paul.

A group has never recorded their own song before.

Someday all music groups will record their own songs.

In January 1963 the Beatles recording of "Please Please Me" reached number one on the UK (United Kingdom) charts. In February they went on their first national tour.

I don't believe all this!

Blimey! I wish there were more police!

In May, on their third tour, they had top billing. It was then that Beatlemania—the fans screaming, fainting, and rioting—began.

In October the Beatles appeared on British TV.

They bloody well better let me in. I've been here all day.

The show was called *Sunday Night at the London Palladium*. The theater was mobbed all day.

When they returned from a successful tour of Sweden, the airport was mobbed.

Blimey! I've never seen anything like this in my life!

In November they appeared on The *Royal Variety Show*. Queen Elizabeth, the Queen Mother, Princess Margaret, and Lord Snowden attended.

Those of you in the cheaper seats clap your hands, and those of you in the expensive seats just rattle your jewelry.

There were 250,000 advance orders for the Beatles' second album, *With the Beatles,* beating Elvis Presley's *Blue Hawaii.*

There were one million advance orders for their single "I Want to Hold Your Hand."

In December after the *Beatles Christmas Show,* the *London Times* called the Beatles "the outstanding English composers of 1963."

The *Sunday Times* called them "the greatest composers since Beethoven."

When the Beatles had four solid hits in America, Brian Epstein booked their first United States visit. Ten thousand fans greeted them at Kennedy Airport.

On February 9, 1964, seventy-three million people watched the Beatles on the *Ed Sullivan Show*.

The Washington Coliseum was jammed for their concert.

After the concert, the British Embassy gave a party for them. One girl cut off a piece of Ringo's hair.

After two sell-out shows at *Carnegie Hall* in New York, the Beatles appeared on a second *Ed Sullivan Show* in Miami Beach.

After it was over, they rested on a private boat.

The police sergeant who was in charge of their security invited them to his house for dinner.

The Beatles were mobbed on their return to England.

How much money is their police protection costing?

It doesn't matter. They are the best export we ever had. I say God bless the Beatles!

Their records were all hits. And so was John Lennon's book *In His Own Write*.

I've already read it but want my own copy.

My mum wants a copy. And so does Granny.

The Beatles toured Europe, Hong Kong, Australia, and New Zealand. They were met by record crowds and screaming fans wherever they went.

All over the world boys were copying the Beatles—their hairdo, the button-down shirts, knitted ties, and Cuban-heeled boots.

In 1964 the Beatles first movie, *A Hard Day's Night,* opened. The reviews were excellent. It was directed by Richard Lester.

They have the kind of magic that the Marx Brothers have.

Movies with pop stars in them have always been poor. This is different. It's original!

A Hard Day's Night was about the Beatles themselves—but making fun of themselves.

It was about how they felt imprisoned by their own success. In the movie they were always being chased by fans; they dealt with reporters' nonsense questions; and they were put down by people in power.

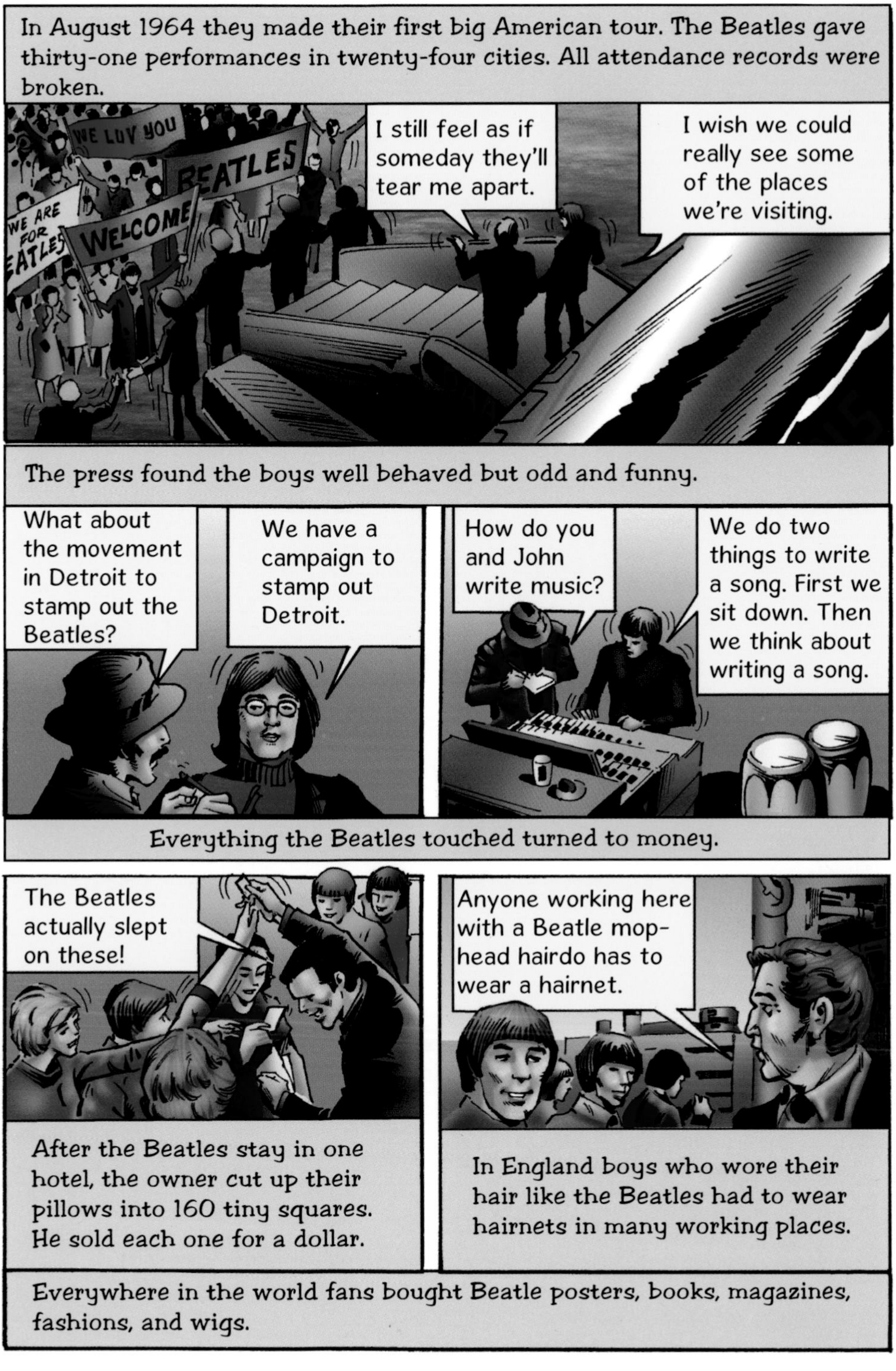
In August 1964 they made their first big American tour. The Beatles gave thirty-one performances in twenty-four cities. All attendance records were broken.
WE LUV YOU
BEATLES
WELCOME
I still feel as if someday they'll tear me apart.
I wish we could really see some of the places we're visiting.
The press found the boys well behaved but odd and funny.
What about the movement in Detroit to stamp out the Beatles?
We have a campaign to stamp out Detroit.
How do you and John write music?
We do two things to write a song. First we sit down. Then we think about writing a song.
Everything the Beatles touched turned to money.
The Beatles actually slept on these!
After the Beatles stay in one hotel, the owner cut up their pillows into 160 tiny squares. He sold each one for a dollar.
Anyone working here with a Beatle mop-head hairdo has to wear a hairnet.
In England boys who wore their hair like the Beatles had to wear hairnets in many working places.
Everywhere in the world fans bought Beatle posters, books, magazines, fashions, and wigs.

After *A Hard Day's Night,* the Beatles musical style changed. They sang more ballads and the music was not as simple.

Their music was praised by Duke Ellington and Leonard Bernstein.

The Beatles were different from most other singers and pop groups. They were liked by almost everyone: males, females, children, parents, and grandparents.

After their 1966 tour of the United States, all the Beatles were millionaires. They loved their fame, but it brought troubles too.

I'm afraid that some fan might pull Zak right out of his pram and kidnap him!

What are you doing here?

We wanted to see John's wife and son.

Ringo married his Liverpool sweetheart, Maureen Cox. They had two sons at the time, Zak and Jason.

In 1965 the Beatles were awarded the MBE, Members of the Most Honorable Order of the British Empire, by England's Queen Elizabeth.

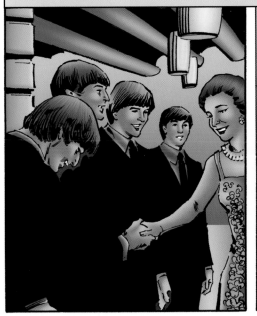

They've brought a lot of money and fame to England.

Just four lucky lads from Liverpool. We export coal but the Queen did not honor the miners with medals.

Many former winners objected to a pop group being so honored. Some sent their medals back.

In August 1965 the Beatles appeared at Shea Stadium in New York. The police were keeping busy by picking up fainting girls.

In December the Beatles made their last personal appearance tour of England.

Also in August 1965 the Beatles movie *Help!* was released. Richard Lester also directed this movie. It was well received and funny but not as successful as *A Hard Day's Night.*

Help! was a take-off of the British spy stories. It centered on a ring that Ringo was wearing. A mad scientist wanted the ring.

In 1966 the Beatles went on a world tour. It was to be their last world tour together.

We love them here!

Everybody loves the Beatles, even when they can't understand their words.

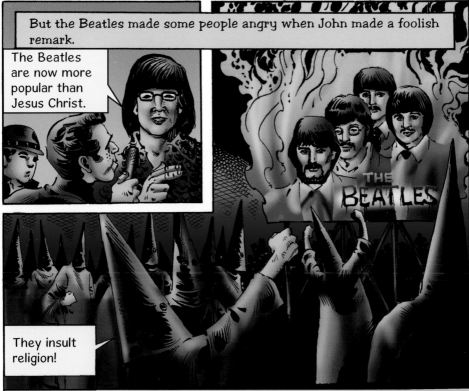

But the Beatles made some people angry when John made a foolish remark.

The Beatles are now more popular than Jesus Christ.

They insult religion!

Then John made a public apology. He explained that he had not meant to be disrespectful.

In 1966 George Harrison married Patti Boyd, a top British model. Later they went to India.

This is what I want to play, a sitar.

How shall we free ourselves?

Meditate every day.

In India, the Harrisons studied with the Maharishi, a well-known religious teacher. Later all the Beatles worked with him.

They continued to produce hit records and songs: *Revolver, Sgt. Pepper's Lonely Hearts Club Band,* "Strawberry Fields Forever," "Being for the Benefit of Mr. Kite," and "Lucy in the Sky with Diamonds."

The lyrics for "Being for the Benefit of Mr. Kite" were taken from an old English music hall poster.

And the lyrics for "Lucy in the Sky with Diamonds" came from my son, Julian. That's what he called one of his drawings.

People try to find meanings in our songs. Sometimes we don't even know what they mean.

In July, 150 million viewers watched the Beatles TV show, *Our World.*

Look, they are using harpsichords and sitars. They're always full of surprises!

Brian Epstein died suddenly in August 1967. The Beatles missed his friendship and management.

In December 1967 *The Magical Mystery Tour* was shown on British TV. Written, directed, and starring the Beatles, the film showed their inexperience in movie-making. Reviews were poor.

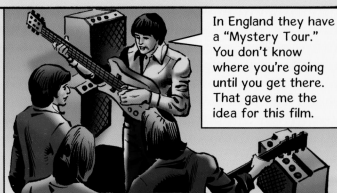

In England they have a "Mystery Tour." You don't know where you're going until you get there. That gave me the idea for this film.

After this TV, show the Beatles announced plans for their new company, Apple Corps. Paul was the head.

We need a business manager.

Aside from recording their own music, they planned to help other people with good ideas.

Apple Corps closed in August 1968. It had been a disappointment.

We were too generous with our money. And the people we trusted were untrained.

In early 1968 all the Beatles went to India to study.

Well, we are not alone. The Maharishi has quite a following: Hollywood movie stars, big shots, and us.

In July 1968 a cartoon movie of the Beatles was released. It was called *The Yellow Submarine.*

This movie showed that music and joy could overcome the enemies of happiness. The Beatles' films were unique.

In 1969 John Lennon was married to Yoko Ono.

Paul McCartney married Linda Eastman, an American photographer.

John has changed. He is interested in strange causes now.

I want to release my solo album *McCartney*.

If you do, it will hurt the sales of *Let It Be*.

More and more, the Beatles were going there separate ways.

I don't like our manager, Allen Klein.

Well, he helped us with our old contract with Epstein.

Let's talk about something nice like our last album *Abbey Road*.

John returned his MBE medal as a protest against the wars in Biafra and Vietnam. He also appeared in an anti-war movie.

In May 1970 the Beatle's movie *Let It Be* was released. None of the Beatles attended the premier. This was a semi-documentary, showing the Beatles working together and fooling around. It also showed John and Paul disagreeing with each other.

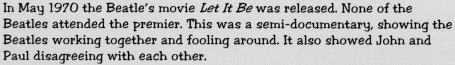

In this scene, let's …

That's a good idea!

They never finish their sentences. Yet they understand each other perfectly!

The Beatles made several albums separately from the group.

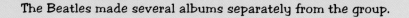

My album *McCartney* is doing well.

And so is my single "Give Peace a Chance."

And now I am a composer too. *All Things Must Pass* is doing okay.

I may not have records, but I am in the movies as an actor.

In December 1970 Paul filed a suit in court demanding that the Beatles no longer be considered a group.

I didn't leave the Beatles. The Beatles have left the Beatles, but no one wants to say the party is over.

Any other group could have gotten a replacement for a member who left. But the Beatles were made up of John Lennon, Paul McCartney, George Harrison, and Ringo Starr. No one else would do.

JOHN LENNON

On December 8, 1980, Lennon was shot and killed in New York City. The 1971 song "Imagine" took on a whole new meaning after his death.

RINGO STARR

Starr is active in music, television, and film. Many drummers today list Ringo as an influence.

GEORGE HARRISON

Harrison died of lung cancer on November 21, 2001. He often said, "Everything else can wait but the search for God cannot wait, and love one another."

PAUL MCCARTNEY

Sir Paul is still active in music: classical, electronic, pop, and film scores. He was knighted by Queen Elizabeth II in 1997.

Saddleback's Graphic Fiction & Nonfiction

If you enjoyed this Graphic Biography ... you will also enjoy our other graphic titles including:

Graphic Classics

- Around the World in Eighty Days
- The Best of Poe
- Black Beauty
- The Call of the Wild
- A Christmas Carol
- A Connecticut Yankee in King Arthur's Court
- Dr. Jekyll and Mr. Hyde
- Dracula
- Frankenstein
- The Great Adventures of Sherlock Holmes
- Gulliver's Travels
- Huckleberry Finn
- The Hunchback of Notre Dame
- The Invisible Man
- Jane Eyre
- Journey to the Center of the Earth
- Kidnapped
- The Last of the Mohicans
- The Man in the Iron Mask
- Moby Dick
- The Mutiny On Board H.M.S. Bounty
- The Mysterious Island
- The Prince and the Pauper
- The Red Badge of Courage
- The Scarlet Letter
- The Swiss Family Robinson
- A Tale of Two Cities
- The Three Musketeers
- The Time Machine
- Tom Sawyer
- Treasure Island
- 20,000 Leagues Under the Sea
- The War of the Worlds

Graphic Shakespeare

- As You Like It
- Hamlet
- Julius Caesar
- King Lear
- Macbeth
- The Merchant of Venice
- A Midsummer Night's Dream
- Othello
- Romeo and Juliet
- The Taming of the Shrew
- The Tempest
- Twelfth Night

SADDLEBACK
EDUCATIONAL PUBLISHING